DATE DUE

Demco, Inc. 38-293

Why did
THE GREAT DEPRESSION
happen?

R. G. GRANT

Gareth Stevens
Publishing

Please visit our Web site, www.garethstevens.com.
For a free color catalog of all our high-quality books,
call toll free 1-800-542-2595 or fax 1-877-542-2596.

Library of Congress Cataloging-in-Publication Data

Grant, R. G.
Why did the Great Depression happen? / R.G. Grant.
    p. cm. -- (Moments in history)
Includes index.
ISBN 978-1-4339-4169-6 (library binding)
ISBN 978-1-4339-4170-2 (pbk.)
ISBN 978-1-4339-4171-9 (6-pack)
1. Depressions--1929--United States--Juvenile literature.
2. Depressions--1929--Europe--Juvenile literature.
3. Stock Market Crash, 1929--Juvenile literature.
4. United States--Economic conditions--1918-1945--
Juvenile literature. 5. Europe--Economic conditions--
1918-1945--Juvenile literature. I. Title.
HB37171929 .G684 2011
330.973'0917--dc22
                        2010012461

First Edition

Published in 2011 by
Gareth Stevens Publishing
111 East 14th Street, Suite 349
New York, NY 10003

Copyright © 2011 Arcturus Publishing

Series concept: Alex Woolf
Editors: Philip de Ste. Croix and Kathy Elgin
Designer: Andrew Easton
Picture researcher: Thomas Mitchell
Project manager: Joe Harris

Photo credits: All the photographs in this book were
supplied by Getty Images, except cover image: Corbis.

Printed in the United States of America

CPSIA compliance information: Batch #AS10GS: For further information contact
Gareth Stevens, New York, New York at 1-800-542-2595.

SL001511US

CONTENTS

1 THE ROOTS OF THE PROBLEM   4

2 BOOM AND BUST   10

3 DEPRESSION TAKES HOLD   18

4 THE LONG FIGHT BACK   26

5 A FALSE DAWN   34

6 A NEW CONFLICT   40

GREAT DEPRESSION TIMELINE   46

GLOSSARY   47

FURTHER INFORMATION   47

INDEX   48

CHAPTER 1

THE ROOTS OF THE PROBLEM

What we now call the Great Depression was a worldwide economic slump, at its worst between 1929 and 1934, that brought about a collapse of international trade and resulted in mass unemployment. Although the Depression is associated with the 1930s, some of the economic and political problems that caused it had their roots in World War I (1914–1918), and would not be fully resolved until World War II (1939–1945).

The capitalist world economy of the early 1900s functioned smoothly, on the whole. As the world's leading trading nation and, effectively, the world's banker, Britain invested capital in many parts of the globe, and used this dominant position to maintain an orderly system of international finance and trade.

The United States and Germany had outstripped Britain and France as the world's major industrial producers, while other countries, such as Russia and Japan, were industrializing rapidly. Asia, Africa, and South America supplied raw materials or food to the industrial countries.

The stable economic system gave businessmen and industrialists the confidence to invest money anywhere in the world, and this investment produced rapid economic growth—new railways, ports, and mines, and the opening up of fresh areas for farming. However, Europe and North America ran the world economy for their own advantage. Pre-1914 society was built

During World War I, the world's leading economic powers directed their industrial and financial resources to the business of destruction. The war claimed the lives of over 9 million soldiers, many of them killed in trench warfare.

The unrest generated by Germany's postwar political and economic crisis was one of the major obstacles to restoring a stable world economy. Here Communist insurgents, known as Spartacists, fight government forces on the streets of Berlin during the winter of 1918–1919.

on radical inequality, and even the richest countries had millions of people living in abject poverty.

WAR INTERVENES

The stable world economy was shattered by the outbreak of World War I. Britain, France, Germany, Russia, and, from 1917, the United States, began to direct their entire economic resources towards the war effort. Governments took unprecedented control over their national economies. After four years of conflict, during which almost 10 million soldiers and uncounted millions of civilians died in Europe, the end of the war saw a defeated Germany in political and economic chaos, with millions of its people on the brink of starvation. Russia had undergone a revolution that

brought a Communist government to power, while Britain and France were virtually bankrupted by the debts they had incurred by borrowing from the United States in order to pay for armaments.

In the aftermath of the war, Europe was plagued by political and social

5

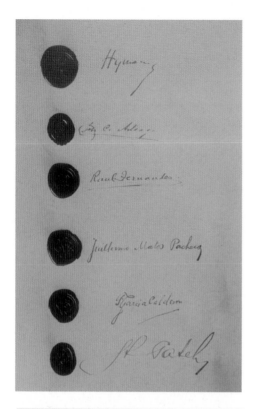

At the peace conference held in France at the end of the war, the various world leaders put their signatures on the Treaty of Versailles. Germany was forced to accede to the terms set down by the victors, but many Germans blamed the treaty for their country's postwar economic and political difficulties.

Hyperinflation hits Germany

In January 1923, France and Belgium, frustrated by Germany's failure to make the reparation payments specified in the Treaty of Versailles, sent troops to occupy the Ruhr district—the industrial heartland of Germany. Unable to offer armed opposition, workers in the occupied area responded with passive resistance: they went on strike. In these chaotic conditions, hyperinflation took off and the value of the German currency collapsed. By November 1923, 600,000 million German marks were worth just one U.S. dollar. It now took 40,000 million marks to buy what one mark would have bought in 1918. People's life savings were wiped out overnight—the 68,000 marks earned in a lifetime's work no longer bought even a postage stamp. Inflation was eventually brought under control in 1924 and a new mark was launched, but the experience of hyperinflation left many Germans bitter and insecure. It also made them more ready to support political extremists in the future.

unrest. Germany was in a state of virtual civil war, with sporadic Communist uprisings and attempted coups by right-wing nationalists through the end of 1923. Russia underwent the horrors of civil war and widespread famine before the Soviet Union, the world's first anticapitalist state, was established at the end of 1922. Foreign businessmen and governments who had invested in Russia before the war lost everything as the Communists renounced the debts of the previous regime.

PAYBACK TIME

The years of conflict were to cast a long shadow over Europe. Even when a certain degree of order had been restored, bitter resentments simmered. The peace treaty of Versailles, imposed by the victorious Allies in 1919, generated widespread hostility in Germany, especially the demand that Germany should compensate the other countries for the cost of the war. However, Britain and France desperately needed these reparation payments, partly in order to pay back their enormous war debts to the United States. Attempts to extract the payments from Germany embittered international relations in the postwar years, and led to hyperinflation in Germany.

DEPRESSION COMES TO BRITAIN

The war had cost Britain its leading position in the world economy. Now a debtor nation, it could no longer expect to dominate the global financial system. Britain was more politically stable than Germany, but her traditional industries of shipbuilding, coal mining, and cotton textile production had never regained their prewar dominance in export markets. By the summer of 1921, 2 million workers were unemployed. By June 1921, according to historian John Stevenson, Britain had already "entered the years of the Depression."

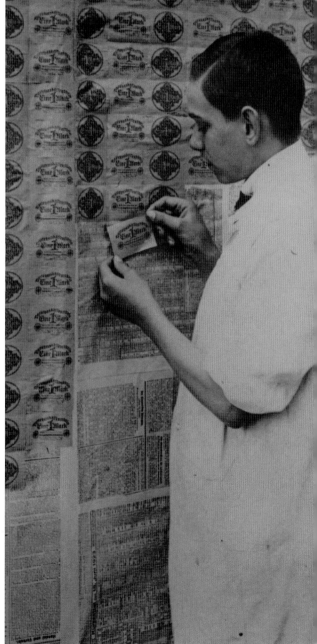

Germany's hyperinflation made banknotes so valueless that people used them to paper their walls. By 1923, people found their cash savings had become almost valueless: a sum set aside for buying a house now barely covered the cost of a streetcar ticket.

These industrial problems were not confined to Britain but were a worldwide concern. While European countries were devoting their economic energies to the war, other countries had stepped in to take their place in the world market. Industrial production for export expanded in Japan and the United States, and in parts of the world ruled by Europeans as colonies—for example, British-ruled India. When the war ended and European industries turned back to producing peacetime goods, there was more industrial capacity worldwide than there was demand. There were not enough customers to buy all the goods that were being produced.

OVERPRODUCTION ON THE FARM

The problem of overproduction in farming was becoming apparent even before the war. New and advanced farming techniques had encouraged

The inaugural meeting of the Council of the League of Nations took place in Geneva, Switzerland, in November 1920. The United States' refusal to join the League seriously undermined its ability to promote future international cooperation.

the turning over of more land to agriculture, but consumer demand did not keep pace with the increase in crops and meat being produced. During the war, countries across the world, including Canada and the United States, increased agricultural production. Once the war was over, however, this high level of production was no longer necessary. As a result, in the 1920s, prices for agricultural goods fell worldwide. Millions of people who worked the land were threatened with poverty.

American farmers suffered in the mounting agricultural crisis of the 1920s. The United States had emerged from the war as the world's leading

WHY DID IT HAPPEN ?

America takes the lead

After World War I, Britain ceded its place as the world's leading financial power to the United States. It has been suggested that America's desire to turn its back on the wider world after the war—isolationism—left the world economy leaderless. Historian Eric Hobsbawm wrote: "The world system, it could be argued, did not work, because, unlike Great Britain, which had been at its centre before 1914, the USA did not much need the rest of the world and, therefore ... did not bother to act as a global stabilizer."

Other historians of the period have disagreed, however. William A. Williams pointed out that the United States involved itself in the wider world in the 1920s out of self-interest, and the U.S. government encouraged lending abroad by American companies and banks to keep the international economy afloat and promote America's export industries.

Eric Hobsbawm, *Age of Extremes* (Michael Joseph, 1994); Williams' views from Charles P. Kindelberger, *The World in Depression 1929–39* (Penguin, 1973)

industrial and financial power. As its industries boomed throughout the 1920s, the United States claimed more than 40 percent of the world's total industrial production.

THE MIGHTY DOLLAR

As the world emerged from war, many in America felt that the best way to maintain their peace and prosperity was to avoid becoming embroiled in the affairs of other countries. This policy of isolationism prompted the United States' refusal to join the League of Nations—the forerunner of the United Nations—in 1920.

America's economic power inevitably gave it great influence in shaping the world economy. In the mid-1920s, an opportunity arose for the world economy to get back on an even keel and achieve what was called at the time a "return to normalcy." In 1924, the American-backed Dawes Plan set out an agreed schedule for German reparation payments, ending the immediate crisis. As investment from American banks and corporations flowed into Germany, the German mark was restored to value after the madness of the great inflation. American investment and American demand for raw materials and foodstuffs also stimulated economic growth around the world.

In 1925, Britain returned to the Gold Standard—a method of fixing the value of a currency by relating each unit to a certain amount of gold. This was seen by many as a return to the orderly prewar world. But the future of the world economy now depended on the United States.

CHAPTER 2

BOOM AND BUST

Between 1922 and 1928, industrial output in the United States rose by 70 percent, an average of 10 percent a year. For many people, these boom years really were "the roaring twenties." New factories opened, existing ones were expanding, and everyone had a job for life. Unemployment was almost unknown.

The major growth area was the production of industrial consumer goods for a mass market. The most striking single example was the automobile. In 1914, there were about half a million cars in the United States; by 1929, there were 26 million—one car for every five citizens. The United States had become the first country in which an average individual could expect to own an automobile. Sales of electrical goods also took off for the first time. Before World War I, fewer than one in five Americans had electricity in their homes, but by 1927 this had risen to one in three. This created a mass market for goods ranging from electric irons and stoves to radios and vacuum cleaners. The United States had become the world's first fully developed consumer society—a society whose central economic activity was the production of what could be termed luxuries for the masses.

The new production-line techniques developed at Henry Ford's automobile factory at Dearborn, Michigan, enabled him to turn out cheap cars for a mass market. In 1929, the last year of the economic boom, the American automobile industry produced 5.6 million cars—about 8 times as many as were manufactured in the whole of Europe.

High above New York, and with no safety harness, a construction worker tightens a bolt on the new Empire State Building. For forty years, it would be the world's tallest building.

Rich and Poor

The American city skyline, with the skyscraper offices of major companies rising in increasing numbers and to ever greater heights, was perhaps the most visible aspect of the country's prosperity. By 1929, New York's Chrysler Building was under construction and the Empire State Building was already on the drawing board. Less visible, however, was the substantial sector of American society that missed out on the boom. For workers in the coal mines of Virginia or African Americans employed in the cotton fields of the South, the 1920s were a time of grinding poverty. While better-off Americans were buying cars and refrigerators, almost a third of the population existed on less than $1,200 a year, a sum then considered the minimum on which a person could reasonably be expected to survive.

Many of the poorest Americans

11

were small farmers or farmhands. As in the rest of the world, agriculture in the United States suffered from overproduction. A combination of factors—including improved crops, new farm machinery, the cultivation of previously unused land, and the expansion of output during World War I—meant that American farmers were producing more than they could easily sell. As a result, the prices they were able to charge for their produce began to fall, especially in the second half of the 1920s. For small farmers, falling prices spelled disaster.

In some ways, a fall in agricultural prices was good for American industry, as it meant cheaper food for workers and cheaper raw materials for factories.

In the cotton fields of Arkansas, African American workers drag in bales of cotton to be weighed. The work was backbreaking, and poorly paid. Workers like these lived in permanent poverty and were little affected by either the boom of the 1920s or the Depression of the 1930s. They just went on being poor.

But the poverty of farmers and farm workers—who made up more than two-fifths of the population—was a serious problem for consumer industries. With no cash to spare, the farmers could not afford to buy the goods the factories were turning out. With a third of Americans too poorly paid to afford automobiles, electrical goods, and other consumer items, it was only a matter of time before the industry ran out of customers.

EASY CREDIT

Another problem was that the boom years were built on the availability of credit. People were only too happy to take advantage of loans at low interest to buy cars and household equipment. Worse, farmers mortgaged their farms to raise loans from banks. By 1929, the debts of American farmers totaled about $10 billion. Obviously, individuals in debt were vulnerable to an economic downturn. But the banks were also at risk. For example, if farmers went bankrupt and their farms became virtually worthless, the banks would lose the money they had lent and might themselves face financial ruin.

The riskiest new activity of all was borrowing money to invest in the stock market. From 1924 to 1929, buying shares seemed a sure way of making money, because share prices constantly went up. On average, over that period they quadrupled in price. At first the rise in share prices was modest and accurately reflected the increasing size or rising profits of businesses. But from 1927 onwards, the rise in the markets turned into sheer speculation. Shares kept on going up in value simply because investors were always prepared to pay more for them, regardless of the success or failure of the businesses the

No one could guess that the stately New York Stock Exchange on Wall Street would become the focus of such a dramatic event as the Crash of 1929. Millions of Americans whose money was invested on Wall Street lost heavily when boom turned to bust.

The scene on Wall Street during the Crash of October 1929. Anxious crowds gathered as the bad news spread, but there was little investors could do but wait as the shares they had bought with their savings dwindled in value.

shares were in. Sharp traders started promoting shares in companies that did no business at all—no one minded paying $5 for a share in a worthless company if they could sell the share to another investor a year later for $10. It was like a casino in which the gamblers never lost.

By 1929, ordinary people were investing their life savings in the stock market, caught up in the fever of making easy money. Some bought shares on margin. This meant paying as little as 10 percent of the share price with their own money and borrowing the rest from a broker—who in turn borrowed the money from a bank. Just $10 could buy you $100 worth of shares. But if the value of the shares

VOICES FROM HISTORY

No laughing matter

One of the famous Marx Brothers comedy team, Harpo, was just one individual caught up in the nightmare of speculation. He had invested every cent he could raise in shares, only to see their value wiped out in the crash. He wrote:

"I had scraped the bottom of the barrel ... liquidated every asset I owned except my harp ... borrowed as far in advance as I could against my salary. My market holdings were probably worth a medium-sized bag of jelly beans."

Quoted in Maury Klein, *Rainbow's End: The Crash of 1929* (Oxford, 2001)

fell, the broker would either demand that the investor put up more money or would sell him out—force him to sell the shares immediately to pay the broker off. This way, any drop in share prices was sure to create an avalanche of forced sales.

THE GOOD TIMES END

By 1929, the mounting agricultural crisis and slowing of industrial growth were sure signs of an inherent weakness in the American economy. But in the fever of speculation on the stock

Hearing that their bank is about to fail, customers rush to withdraw their money. Thousands of banks found themselves with no funds to repay people the money that they had put into their savings accounts.

The sight of unemployed Americans lining up for charity handouts of food or used clothing became common in 1930. The millions of workers laid off by failing businesses were left to survive on relief payments from city authorities, or food and other essentials provided by charitable organizations.

exchange, all the warning signs were ignored. March 1929 saw a slight drop in the market, but after this "wobble," speculation renewed at an ever more intense pitch. On September 3, another brief, sharp fall in share prices was quickly reversed. But by mid-October, selling of shares had begun in earnest. Despite the reassuring statements of prominent American financiers who tried to calm the situation, declining confidence turned to panic. On Black Thursday, October 24, there was a torrent of selling. Everyone wanted to sell shares but no one wanted to buy. Share prices fell steeply as panicking investors sold for whatever they could get. Over the next few days, there were hopes that prices might recover, but on October 29, Black Tuesday, over 16 million shares were sold, many for next to nothing.

TURNING POINTS IN HISTORY

Black Thursday

The catastrophic crash of the American stock market began late on Wednesday, October 23, 1929, with heavy selling of shares. When the market opened at 10:00 a.m. the next day, 1.6 million shares were sold in half an hour. That day became known as Black Thursday. Rumors of ruined speculators committing suicide ran through the anxious crowds filling the streets outside the New York Stock Exchange. People's shocked faces showed, in the words of one eyewitness, "the dazed unbelief of men who have been robbed of their all."

Cause and effect

There is a difference of opinion between economists and historians as to the relationship between the Great Crash and the Depression. Some see the Crash as a spectacular side-effect of the onset of the Depression, believing that shares fell in value because the American economy was already going into decline. Economist Thomas Wilson, for example, wrote that the fall in share prices "reflected, in the main, the change which was already apparent in the industrial situation."

Others see the Crash as a primary cause of the Depression through its undermining of public confidence. Historian Maury Klein wrote: "The real problem lay ... in the hearts and minds of the American people. The crash had struck a deadly, perhaps fatal blow [to] the American psyche."

The economic historian J. K. Galbraith took up a position midway between these views: "Had the economy been fundamentally sound in 1929 the effect of the great stock market crash might have been small ... But business in 1929 was not sound; on the contrary it was exceedingly fragile. It was vulnerable to the kind of blow it received from Wall Street."

Wilson and Gilbraith quotes from J. K. Galbraith, *The Great Crash 1929* (Hamish Hamilton, 1955); Maury Klein, *Rainbow's End: The Crash of 1929* (Oxford, 2001)

THE GREAT CRASH

The sudden collapse in share prices, known as "The Great Crash," shocked the American public. Many thousands of individuals who had put all their savings into shares—or, even worse, had borrowed money to buy shares—faced financial ruin as these shares became worthless. Financial experts, however, saw the fall in prices as simply restoring share prices to a realistic level after a wave of speculation, and continued to speak calmly of a "market correction." Figures showed that, on average, the crash only returned shares to the previous year's value. Nor was it obvious that the United States was entering a major economic crisis. The fall in industrial output in 1930 and the sharp rise in unemployment were at first seen as merely a temporary situation. When President Herbert Hoover stated in May 1930 that America had "passed the worst," he was expressing a widespread expectation that the economy would soon pick up again.

But neither the American stock market nor the American economy recovered. Instead, industrial output went on falling, unemployment went on rising, and share prices plummeted ever further. By mid-1932, the average value of shares was a quarter of the level it had held at the end of 1929. The confidence in a bright future that had underscored the 1920s boom was gone. The Great Depression had arrived.

CHAPTER 3

DEPRESSION TAKES HOLD

In the opening years of the new decade, the American economy went into free fall. For the first time, mass unemployment swept the United States as, one after another, factories shut down. At the end of 1930, around 5 million Americans were out of work, but just two years later unemployment had risen to over 12 million—one in four of the working population. Those lucky enough to keep their jobs faced wage cuts or a reduction to part-time work. Spending on consumer goods plummeted as people cut back on nonessential purchases. Between 1929 and 1932, sales of cars halved, while sales of electrical goods fell by around two-thirds. Meanwhile, the price of agricultural produce went into an ever steeper fall, bringing a wave of bankruptcies among farmers. The American banking system was based on a large number of small banks, many with inadequate resources, and as more and more people defaulted on loans and confidence slumped, the whole system neared collapse. Over 1,000 banks failed in 1930 alone.

In rural America, families who had lost their homes tried to hold on to the car. Sometimes it was all they had to live in. Farm workers were among those worst hit by the Depression, and many of their children grew up knowing nothing but poverty.

In Britain, unemployed men line up to receive unemployment benefits. In order to receive these payments from the state, those out of work had to sign in regularly at the "labor exchange," signifying that they were available for work, even though there were no jobs to be had.

EUROPE FEELS THE PINCH

In Europe, too, industrial output fell sharply in the early 1930s and unemployment rose. Germany, whose economic recovery in the 1920s had been based on American loans, was worst affected. With their own economy in crisis, Americans no longer had spare cash to invest abroad. When the American money was pulled out, German industrial output plummeted and the economy collapsed. Unemployment in Germany rose to 3 million in 1929 and by 1931 was standing at around 5 million. In Britain, the effect was less dramatic because that country had not enjoyed quite the same boom in the 1920s. Nevertheless, British unemployment climbed from 2 million in 1929 to 3 million in 1931.

Inevitably, the slump in the industrialized states of Europe and North America had a serious effect on those countries that supplied them with raw materials or foodstuffs—countries which in many cases had already been hit by falling prices. As industries cut back on production they needed fewer

---

VOICES FROM HISTORY

The knock-on effect

In Chile, South America, thousands worked in the copper mines, producing copper for export to the United States. When the Depression hit the U.S., the export market dried up and the mines closed down. A Chilean miner expressed his sense of shock:

"The crisis took us by surprise. It was as if you were walking in the street and something hits you and you are simply stunned. New York was far away, but when your own patron [boss] tells you that you no longer have a job, that the work's over, well that's the moment you go into shock."

Quoted in Godfrey Hodgson, *People's Century* (BBC Books, 1995)

Members of the Nazi Party in Germany listen intently to a speech by their leader, Adolf Hitler. A charismatic speaker, Hitler won the support of millions of Germans in the early 1930s because his extreme nationalist policies promised to solve the problems of Germany's economic collapse and mass unemployment.

imported raw materials, while hard-up consumers bought less imported food, drinks, or luxury products. Workers in the Japanese silk industry found themselves out of work because fewer American women were buying silk stockings. In Brazil, where coffee was produced for export, so much remained unsold that coffee beans were used as fuel for steam locomotives on the railways.

A Difficult Balance

Although the depression was spreading around the world, there was no attempt at a coordinated international response. In fact, most economic experts considered occasional short-term slumps as a natural function of a capitalist economy and they seemed reluctant to admit that anything unusual was happening. They simply advised governments to balance their budgets, which meant making sure that expenditure equaled the income from taxes and dues, and keep the value of the national currency fixed. If all countries did this, the world would soon pull out of the depression and resume economic growth.

So the reaction of governments to falling output and mounting unemployment was generally to cut spending and raise taxes in order to keep national finances stable. But balancing budgets in a depression was difficult because reduced economic activity meant reduced income from taxes. At the same time, rising unemployment meant that in countries such as Britain and Germany, which had state unemployment benefit plans, governments had to spend more to meet the cost of benefits.

The worsening economic situation inevitably put a strain on political systems as the ruling parties struggled to cope with the crisis. In South America, the governments of 10 countries were overthrown in two years. In Germany, political life, which had been temporarily stabilized during the years of relative prosperity in 1924–28, was once more torn apart as both the Communists and Adolf Hitler's right-wing nationalist Nazis attracted mass support by proposing radical solutions to the economic crisis.

EUROPE'S FINANCES IN CRISIS

In May 1931, the Austrian Creditanstalt bank closed down, bringing the crisis in Europe dramatically to a head during that spring and summer. The Creditanstalt was by far the largest

Unemployed men support a woman injured during a demonstration against job losses in Bristol, England, in February 1932.

The Invergordon mutiny

Faced with a mounting financial crisis, in September 1931 the British government introduced spending cuts. Everyone paid by the state was to have their income slashed. This included teachers, whose pay was reduced by 15 percent; the unemployed, whose benefits were cut by 10 percent; and members of the armed forces, some of whom faced a 25 percent pay cut. On September 15, sailors at the Royal Navy's Invergordon base in Scotland refused duty in protest of the cuts. This was mutiny, and when news of it spread, it undermined what little confidence the world still had in Britain. As foreign investors withdrew their money, the value of the pound fell. The government was unable to resist this financial pressure and was forced to abandon the sacred gold standard. The value of the pound dropped by a quarter on foreign exchange markets. But the naval action had achieved one thing: the government announced that all pay and benefit cuts would be limited to a maximum of 10 percent, and after two days the sailors quietly returned to duty.

bank in Austria, controlling investment in most of the country's industry. Its collapse sent panic sweeping through Germany and Central Europe as people rushed to withdraw their money from banks they feared might go under. In the summer of 1931, the financial crisis engulfed Britain. In August, British prime minister Ramsay MacDonald established a coalition national government to push through spending cuts. Even so, Britain was forced to abandon the gold standard, the mechanism that fixed the value of the pound. When other countries followed Britain's lead, it was clear that the battle to uphold a world economic system based on fixed exchange rates and stable currencies had been lost.

Once the gold standard was

Republican President Herbert Hoover took action to boost the economy, but failed to halt rising unemployment or relieve poverty. By the election year of 1932, Hoover appeared to many Americans as both heartless and incompetent.

VOICES FROM HISTORY

Fathers and sons

Larry Van Dusen, a teenager during the Depression, reveals how his father's unemployment blighted family life:

"One of the most common things—and it certainly happened to me—was this feeling of your father's failure. That somehow he hadn't beaten the rap. Sure, things were tough, but why should I be the kid who had to put a piece of cardboard into the sole of my shoe to go to school? ... The shock, the confusion, the hurt that many kids felt about their fathers not being able to provide for them ... reflected itself very often in bitter quarrels between father and son."

Quoted in Studs Terkel, *Hard Times* (Pantheon Books, 1986)

abandoned, the value of one national currency against another—for example, how many U.S. dollars were equivalent to a certain number of British pounds— was no longer fixed and predictable. As a result, it was much more difficult for importers in one country to pay for goods from another country. This was a major factor in the collapse in world trade, which shrank by an astonishing 60 percent between 1929 and 1933. A bad situation was made worse by the imposition of tariffs. These were taxes levied by countries on imported goods, and their purpose, apart from raising revenue, was to protect a nation's industry and agriculture from foreign competition by making the imported goods more expensive to buy. The

These makeshift shacks in shantytowns on the outskirts of cities were known as "Hoovervilles," after the president who was held responsible for the depressed state of the economy.

United States led the way with the Smoot-Hawley Tariff Act of 1930, which imposed heavy tariffs on agricultural imports in the hope of protecting hard-pressed American farmers. Almost all other countries followed suit, imposing their own tariffs. This has been described as a "beggar-my-neighbor" policy—an attempt to improve the situation of one's own country at the expense of everyone else's. It was a sign that, in the absence of any coordinated international response to the economic crisis, each country was going to seek its own national solution.

PRESIDENT HOOVER'S RESPONSE

This was certainly true in the United States. In 1930, President Hoover had taken positive action to boost the economy by cutting taxes and trying to persuade businessmen to halt wage cuts, so that people would have more money to spend. The following year he set up the Reconstruction Finance Corporation, providing federal money to boost construction projects and prop up banks. Federal cash was also provided to buy surplus farm produce in an effort to halt the fall in farm prices. But Hoover also wanted to balance the federal budget and maintain the value of the dollar. To this end, in 1932 he raised taxes and interest rates and cut spending, even though the Depression was still deepening.

By 1932, it was obvious that America was in the grip of a major crisis. It was visible in the shantytowns—dubbed

"Hoovervilles"—that had sprung up across the United States to house people who had been evicted from their homes because they could no longer afford the rent, and in bankrupted small farmers whose mortgaged farms had been repossessed by banks. "Panhandlers" begged on the streets for small change, and thousands of "hobos," many of them teenagers who had left home to avoid being a burden on the family finances, traveled illegally on freight trains as they roamed the country in search of temporary work.

Society in Crisis

Most major European countries operated some form of nationwide unemployment benefit or welfare payments that alleviated the situation somewhat. In the United States, however, there was no federal system. The poor and unemployed had to depend on charities, or on state or city authorities. Hoover was opposed to giving government money to the unemployed. But charities and local authorities could not cope with a situation in which 12–13 million people were out of work. At all levels of government, falling revenues resulting from the Depression fueled a mounting financial crisis. By 1932, many public authorities lacked the resources to pay the wages of teachers, let alone relief payments for the unemployed. When relief failed, poverty was acute. A woman in Chicago in 1932 witnessed "fifty men fighting over a barrel of garbage outside the back door of a restaurant."

In the summer of 1932, the mounting sense of anger and betrayal felt by a large sector of American society found dramatic expression in the Bonus

One attempt at relief was giving the unemployed boxes of surplus apples to sell on the street. Married women were first to be laid off when job cuts loomed, as there was prejudice against married women working, but sometimes the mother was the only family breadwinner.

Did government get it right?

The British economist John Maynard Keynes, writing in the 1930s, argued that government policies of cutting spending and raising taxes had actually made the Depression much worse. The main cause of the Depression, he maintained, was the lack of demand for manufactured goods. Governments should have cut taxes and increased spending to stimulate the economy, even if this meant failing to balance their budgets.

However, this view has been hotly contested by advocates of liberal capitalism, such as the American economist Milton Friedman. They argue that the Depression was unnecessarily harsh and prolonged because various instances of government interference prevented the natural workings of a capitalist economy which would otherwise have soon restored prosperity.

Almost all critics agree, though, that policy makers in the early 1930s had little idea of how to respond to the crisis. As historian Eric Hobsbawm wrote: "Never did a ship founder with a captain and crew more ignorant of the reasons for its misfortune or more impotent to do anything about it."

Eric Hobsbawm, *Industry and Empire* (Penguin, 1968)

Unarmed army veterans are overwhelmed by the government troops, with rifles and gas masks, sent to clear the Bonus Marchers out of Washington, D.C., in July 1932. The shantytown shacks were also burned and bulldozed.

Army protest. This was organized by war veterans who had fought in the U.S. Army during World War I and were now unemployed. They were demanding immediate payment of a bonus that had been granted to them by the government in 1924, but was not scheduled to be paid in full until 1945. The protesters and their families, more than 10,000 strong, set up camp in Washington, D.C., vowing not to leave until the bonus was paid. Hoover and the U.S. Congress were equally determined not to pay up. On July 28, the U.S. Army was ordered to attack the Bonus Army encampment and drive the protesters out.

This whole episode confirmed the public's growing conviction that Hoover was not only ill equipped to deal with the economic crisis, but heartless in his response to people's suffering. In the presidential election the following autumn, they voted in droves for Hoover's opponent, Democratic candidate Franklin D. Roosevelt.

CHAPTER 4

THE LONG FIGHT BACK

Overwhelmingly the people's choice in the 1932 election, Franklin D. Roosevelt was inaugurated as president on March 3, 1933. He had fought the election on a platform of two main promises. One was to repeal Prohibition, the law banning alcohol that had been in place since 1919. The other was to introduce a "New Deal" to conquer the Depression, and to concern himself with "the forgotten man at the bottom of the economic pyramid." Prohibition was easily dealt with by passing a new law: coping with the Depression was another matter.

Roosevelt and his advisers held contradictory ideas of how to get America back to work. For example, Roosevelt was very conservative in his attitude to public finance. One of his first acts as president was to cut the wages of federal employees in an effort to balance the budget. Yet his New Deal policies led to a sharp rise in federal spending and a totally unplanned budget deficit.

THE GREAT COMMUNICATOR

Although not skilled in economics, the new president brought to the White House immense dynamism, an openness

President Franklin D. Roosevelt speaks directly to the American people in one of his famous "fireside chats." Through these revolutionary radio broadcasts, Roosevelt projected a personal warmth that gave many Americans comfort and renewed confidence in difficult times.

to fresh thinking and initiatives of all kinds, and a human warmth that inspired confidence. His regular radio broadcasts, or "fireside chats," were delivered in an intimate, relaxed style that created an immediate bond with the millions of listening Americans. As a Chicago doctor said later: "It was the hopeful voice of FDR that got this thing out of the swamps."

From the outset, Roosevelt displayed a flair for influencing the national mood. In March 1933, America was in the depths of a major banking crisis. All over the country people were storming banks, desperate to withdraw savings in case the bank failed. Many states had closed their banks in an attempt to halt these panic withdrawals. In a deliberately dramatic gesture, Roosevelt's first act on assuming the presidency was to declare a nationwide "bank holiday." Every bank in the United States was closed, and a law was rushed through Congress stating that none would be allowed to reopen unless the federal authorities were sure that it was reliable. Roosevelt then went on the radio to assure the American people that it was now safe to deposit their money. Over the following weeks, almost all banks reopened and confidence was restored.

KICK-STARTING GROWTH

The immediate challenge was to rekindle economic growth by reversing the downward spiral of prices and wages, both in agriculture and in industry. The federal government tried to persuade farmers to reduce surpluses and halt falling prices by limiting

> ### VOICES FROM HISTORY
>
> ## A stirring speech
> The words of Roosevelt's inauguration speech have gone down in history. He told the American people:
>
> *"Let me assert my firm belief that the only thing we have to fear is fear itself—nameless, unreasoning, unjustified terror which paralyses needed efforts to convert retreat into advance."* The speech ended with Roosevelt announcing his intention of asking Congress *"for broad executive powers to wage a war against the emergency, as great as the power that would be given to me if we were in fact invaded by a foreign foe."*
>
> Quoted in Martin Gilbert, *A History of the Twentieth Century* (HarperCollins, 1997)

production. Cotton farmers were paid to take land out of cultivation, and millions of piglets were slaughtered to prevent a glut of pork. In industry, the new National Recovery Administration (NRA) tried to persuade businesses to stop cutting wages and prices, and to abandon certain bad practices, such as employing child labor. Across the United States, businesses agreed to implement the voluntary codes, displaying the NRA's Blue Eagle badge to indicate that they were following the new rules.

In practice, the New Deal industrial and agricultural recovery policies had limited effect. The NRA encouraged large businesses to make price-fixing agreements that guaranteed their

Cartoonists were kept busy during the Depression. "Spirit of the New Deal," from 1933, shows how the National Recovery Administration (NRA) was supposed to work, with employers and employees brought together in the warm embrace of Uncle Sam.

Unprecedented legislation

During the first 100 days of Roosevelt's presidency—from the second week in March to mid-June 1933—Congress passed more new legislation than in any similar period before or since. This included the Emergency Banking Act, aimed at restoring confidence in the banking system, and the Farm Relief Act, intended to tackle the crisis in agriculture. Other acts established the Civilian Conservation Corps, providing work for the young unemployed; the Public Works Administration, promoting major construction projects; the Tennessee Valley Authority, set up to develop a depressed region of the South; and the National Recovery Administration, intended to get industry back on its feet. A journalist at the time described all these initiatives as a "whirlwind of changes in the old order." Whatever their practical impact, they created an impression of dynamism that helped lift the mood of the American nation.

profits, discouraging them from competing with one another. They took advantage of this while largely ignoring pressure to improve wages and working conditions. In agriculture, large-scale farmers profited from government payments but there was no improvement for the owners of small farms or tenant farmers. Overall, the first four years of Roosevelt's presidency saw gradual economic recovery, with growth of about 10 percent a year, but this was not enough to solve the problem of mass unemployment. By 1937, one in eight Americans was still looking for a job.

CREATING WORK

With mass unemployment still a major problem, it was crucial that New Deal measures were aimed directly at benefiting the unemployed. One of Roosevelt's first acts was to provide federal funding to boost bankrupt state and city unemployment relief programs. Although the amount of relief varied enormously depending on where people lived, the provision of federal funds was a lifeline for many.

The government also launched large-scale federal work programs for the unemployed. The Civilian Conservation Corps (CCC) was exclusively for young people and, at its height, put 2.5 million youths to work on rural projects such as tree planting. The Civil Works Administration (CWA) and the Works Progress Administration (WPA) provided employment for adults, primarily in construction work

These young people are on a tree-planting program at a Civilian Conservation Corps (CCC) camp in Virginia. The CCC was one of the more successful of the New Deal initiatives, giving millions of young unemployed Americans something useful to do, as well as benefiting the environment.

and road-building but also in civic capacities, such as running libraries and theaters, or painting murals in public buildings. These were large scale programs: in January 1934 the CWA alone was employing more than 4 million people. Although undoubtedly some of the work they provided was a "boondoggle"—a word coined to describe a pointless and unnecessary job—the New Deal programs restored a sense of worth and purpose to millions of unemployed people, as well as paying well above what they would have received on welfare.

However, Roosevelt's policies met with a good deal of opposition, partly from people who wanted him to be more radical, but more particularly

Work begins on building one of the dams that were a central feature of the Tennessee Valley Authority (TVA) program. This scheme, one of the major initiatives launched under the New Deal, would bring electricity to regenerate a large area of the rural southern states.

VOICES FROM HISTORY

Thanks, Mr. President

The first paycheck for working on a New Deal program meant a lot to men who had been unemployed for years. Hank Oettinger from Wisconsin remembered the day he got his:

"It was on a Friday. Everyone had gotten his [pay] check. The first check a lot of them had in three years ... I never saw such a change of attitude. Instead of walking around feeling dreary and looking sorrowful, everybody was joyous ... They had money in their pockets for the first time. If Roosevelt had run for president the next day, he'd have gone in by 100 percent."

Studs Terkel, *Hard Times* (Pantheon Books, 1986)

from the wealthy and from big business. He was criticized for extending the size and power of the federal administration. By 1935, the Supreme Court had declared several New Deal policies— including the NRA—unconstitutional, and they had to be abandoned. Undeterred, Roosevelt pressed ahead with a fresh wave of even more radical legislation in 1935. New measures in this Second New Deal included the

Wagner Act, which gave federal support to workers joining trade unions, and the Social Security Act, which introduced old-age pensions and welfare benefits. In the presidential election of 1936, the American people had their chance to pass judgment on the New Deal.

President Roosevelt, seen here acknowledging the applause at his second inauguration in 1937, was one of America's most popular leaders. He served a total of four terms in office, from 1932–1944.

Roosevelt won an overwhelming majority of the popular vote.

THE RISE OF THE NAZIS

Roosevelt was not the only new leader to come to power in 1933 with a commitment to ending unemployment. Adolf Hitler brought his Nazi Party into power when he was elected Chancellor of Germany in January. His economic policies were in some ways similar to those of the American New Deal. Large-scale, state-funded construction projects—including the building of the first Autobahnen (motorways)—provided work, while an

Adolf Hitler reviews the official opening of construction work on a new motorway, one of the state-funded projects that generated employment in Germany after the Nazis came to power in 1933.

31

Regular five-year economic plans were a common feature of the Soviet Union in the 1930s. Here the progress being made in fulfilling the objectives of the latest one is advertised on a billboard for all to see.

intensive program of propaganda set out to restore public confidence in the future. However, Nazi policy differed sharply from Roosevelt's New Deal in its emphasis on military spending. Hitler's expansion of Germany's armed forces not only employed men as soldiers but created thousands of new jobs in armaments factories.

Another crucial difference was that Hitler imposed a dictatorship and implemented his policies by force. Independent trade unions were brutally suppressed and their leaders sent to concentration camps. In 1935, unemployment was made illegal. Any man without a job was conscripted into compulsory National Labor Service, working on the land or building military installations. Women were pressured to leave their jobs and return to what Nazis saw as their proper place in the home, freeing up jobs for men. Jews, whom the Nazis blamed for all of Germany's misfortunes, were forced out of good jobs, which were given to other Germans. Although based on the loss of political freedom, Nazi policies unquestionably solved the problem of unemployment, and to many Germans in the 1930s this seemed like an economic miracle. Hitler was increasingly regarded as the savior of his people.

Country	Change in industrial output 1929–32
France	- 25.6%
Germany	- 40.8%
Italy	- 22.7%
UK	- 11.4%
USA	- 44.7%
USSR	+ 66.7%

The New Deal: radical or conservative?

Historian Barton Bernstein wrote that: "The New Deal ... failed to raise the impoverished, it failed to redistribute income, to extend equality..." This opinion is shared by other left-wing historians, who argue that the New Deal was too conservative, intent on rescuing big business at the expense of the poor. But as others point out, Roosevelt himself always claimed to have conservative aims, stating in 1936: "It was this administration which saved the system of private profit and free enterprise after it had been dragged to the brink of ruin..."

Historian Carl Degler, however, asserts that the New Deal was radical—even revolutionary—in an American context, because of the way it extended the scope of government. Degler says the New Deal made the state into "a vigorous and dynamic force in society energizing and, if necessary, supplanting private enterprise when the general welfare required it." The New Deal has also been praised for its social inclusiveness. David M. Kennedy writes that Roosevelt gave countless Americans "a sense of security, and with it a sense of having a stake in their country."

Barton Bernstein, *Towards a New Past* (Pantheon, New York, 1968); Carl Degler, *Out of Our Past* (Harper & Row, 1984); David M. Kennedy, *Freedom from Fear* (Oxford University Press, 1999)

STALIN'S RUSSIA

The Soviet Union, under Communist dictator Joseph Stalin, found its own answers to the Depression in rapid industrialization and urbanization. In the 1930s, the Soviet capital, Moscow, was the world's fastest-growing city. The Soviet economy was organized by the state, which directed resources and workers to the fulfilment of ambitious production targets laid down in a series of four- or five-year economic plans. Just as in Nazi Germany, unemployment was a crime.

In stark contrast to the sharp falls in industrial production experienced by capitalist countries, in the Soviet Union production grew during the 1930s, promoting the belief that the Communist system was superior to capitalism. But although Soviet industrial growth was real, it was bought at an appalling cost. Millions of Soviet citizens died in mass famines and millions more were used as slave labor in concentration camps. The conditions in which ordinary Soviet citizens lived and worked were far worse than those of average workers in Western Europe or North America. But even if the Communist success of the 1930s was largely an illusion, the idea that capitalism had failed was understandable. Although different national governments adopted different economic policies, they had all given up on attempts to recreate the stable, harmonious global capitalist economy that had existed before 1914. The conditions created by the Depression had been accepted as the new normality.

CHAPTER 5

A FALSE DAWN

Slowly, the world began to emerge from the Depression. By 1934, the worst appeared to be over. Economists had predicted that recovery would eventually happen no matter what policies governments pursued, and this seemed to be the case. In Britain, where no radical economic policies had been launched to combat the slump, a sharp rebound brought industrial output back up to the level of the 1920s. It is probable, too, that the fall in unemployment seen in Germany and the United States between 1933 and 1935 could be put down to a spontaneous recovery in economic activity—a natural consequence of what economists call "economic cycles"—rather than to the New Deal or Hitler's policies.

WORLD TRADE

However welcome the recovery, the problems of mass unemployment and depressed world trade still remained to be solved. Throughout the 1930s, world trade stayed far below the level it had been at before the Depression. There was no restoration of a unified world economy based on free trade and national currencies with a fixed value, as had been the case with the gold standard. A World Economic Conference, held in London in 1933, was doomed to failure by the United States' refusal to participate in a plan to restore the fixed value of currencies, which would have

New Zealand depended on its wool and lamb exports, but during the 1930s, sheep farmers like these could only sell their produce to Britain or other countries within the British empire. Trading outside the area that used British currency was almost impossible.

VOICES FROM HISTORY

Britain on the Dole

In 1933, visiting Hebburn, a town on the River Tyne in northern England, author J. B. Priestley wrote:

"Idle men—and not unemployable casual labourers but skilled men—hung about the streets, waiting for Doomsday. Nothing, it seemed, would ever happen here again ... It is not merely that two-thirds of the town is living on the edge of destitution, tightening its belt another notch every month or two, but that its self-respect is vanishing..."

J. B. Priestley, *English Journey* (Heinemann, 1934)

One of the most heartbreaking sights of 1936 was the march of unemployed men from the town of Jarrow in northern England to London in protest of long-term unemployment in their area.

eased international trade.

America was not alone in turning its back on a search for economic progress based on international cooperation. Those countries with extreme nationalist governments were openly opposed to the return of free trade. The Nazi regime sought to make Germany as economically self-sufficient as possible, producing everything necessary to satisfy its own needs. Where this was not possible, goods were imported from countries that Germany directly or indirectly dominated. Some eastern European countries, including Romania, were made to sign trade deals in which they agreed to supply Germany with essential materials such as oil and foodstuffs in return for German industrial goods. The other countries were in no position to refuse, for fear of Germany's military might.

Even Britain and France, countries which in principle still believed in the

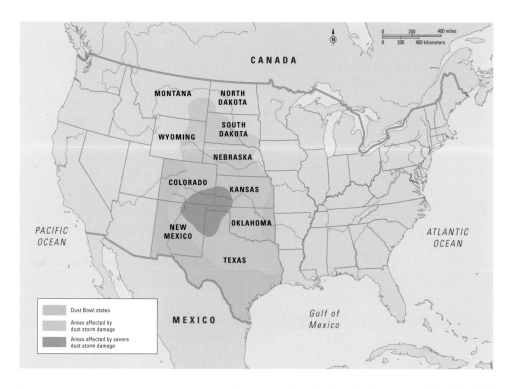

The Dust Bowl was an ecological and economic disaster created by a combination of nature and bad farming practices. Overcultivation of the land, followed by drought, allowed wind to erode topsoil across a swathe of the Great Plains, creating an arid area impossible to farm.

restoration of world trade, in practice no longer traded freely. Britain's dealings were largely restricted to countries that would conduct transactions in sterling, the British currency. Britain made its overseas empire into a protected trade area, ensuring that countries within the empire not only exported most of their produce to Britain but also bought most of their imported goods from Britain.

UNEMPLOYMENT PERSISTS

The failure of world trade to recover during the 1930s was matched by the continuing mass unemployment. Britain was finding it hard to reduce the high levels of unemployment that persisted in parts of the country dependent on industries such as coal mining, shipbuilding, and cotton textiles. In towns such as Jarrow in northern England, most of the population was without work for years on end. The plight of the British unemployed was effectively publicized in 1936 by a march of 200 men from Jarrow to London to deliver a petition to parliament. But although the marchers were regarded with great sympathy, they failed to persuade Britain's political leaders to take radical action.

In the United States, unemployment not only persisted but actually worsened again during Roosevelt's second term in office. In the second half of 1937, American industry experienced a sharp recession. In some areas, such as automobile manufacturing and steel production, much of the gain made in the post-1933 recovery was lost in a few months. As industrial production fell, unemployment rose. Although production picked up somewhat in the last two years of the decade, 1939 saw 9 million unemployed in the United States, compared with 12–13 million when the New Deal began in the depths of the Depression in 1933.

While this high unemployment reflected the failure of American industry to make a true recovery, the problems of American agriculture were just as acute. Some of the country's worst poverty was seen among African American rural workers in the southern United States. Tenant farmers, who did

A migrant worker and her children sit grimly in a camp in California where, like many others, she had gone in search of work picking fruit. This is just one of many photographs taken by Dorothea Lange, who was employed by the Farm Security Administration to document the suffering of America's rural poor. There was no shortage of material.

TURNING POINTS IN HISTORY

The Dust Bowl

The Dust Bowl, made infamous in the ballads of folksinger Woody Guthrie, was an area of the southern Great Plains. Oklahoma and Kansas in particular suffered from years of intensive farming on relatively poor soil, which made the topsoil vulnerable to wind erosion during the frequent droughts. In the early 1930s, a series of massive dust storms stripped the soil from much of the area. One storm, in May 1934, carried dust as far as the distant cities of Boston and New York. The once-valued farmland became a Dust Bowl where nothing would grow. Around 300,000 farmers—known as "Okies" after the Oklahoma they had left—were forced to migrate west towards California in search of work.

not own their own land, had a tough time in the 1930s. The fate of the "Okies," who migrated from the plains of the Oklahoma Dust Bowl to find badly paid work as fruit-pickers in the orchards of California, was especially harsh. The Farm Security Administration (FSA), set up in 1937 to tackle rural poverty, gave loans to poor farmers and provided housing for "Okies" in California. But it was not enough, and many of the rural poor found their own solution by flocking to the cities. In particular, the migration of African Americans from the rural south to the northern cities grew in scale through the 1920s and 1930s.

Winds of Change

Another outcome of America's experience of the Depression and the New Deal was the spread of radical ideas and political action. Millions joined trade unions for the first time, and there were widespread strikes over pay, working conditions, and the unions' right to recognition by employers. In 1937, some 400,000 Americans were involved in sitdown strikes, in which they occupied the workplace. Despite the government's general support for unions, it was not unusual for strikers to be attacked by armed strikebreakers in the pay of the employers, or by police and the National Guard sent in by state or city authorities.

Life, however, was not always grim, and for America the 1930s held more than political conflict, unemployment, and poverty. It was also a time of great technological progress. A more widespread use of electricity, the

The year 1936–37 saw a wave of sitdown strikes, usually hard-fought, and with outbreaks of violence between strikers and police or vigilantes paid by the employers. These workers occupying the General Motors plant in Flint, Michigan, are making clear their hostility to "scabs," who refuse to join the strike. The dummy hanging from the window represents their view on company "stools," or "stool pigeons," paid to spy on the strikers.

New industries expanded in southern England and the Midlands—like this Hoover factory in west London—while old industrial areas remained in the grip of depression.

introduction of plastics and nylon goods, and movies with color and sound brought real improvement to many people's lives. The low prices that spelled poverty for the world's farmers meant cheaper imported food for town and city dwellers with jobs. In Britain, as the old industries of shipbuilding and cotton textiles declined, new industries were springing up, mostly in the Midlands and the south, producing cars, electrical goods, and aircraft. On the whole, workers in the new industries were better paid and better housed than working people had been a generation earlier.

Essentially, by the late 1930s, the world was adapting to the new conditions the Depression had brought, and getting on with its business. There seemed no reason why high unemployment and shrunken world trade should not continue into the future. Some of Roosevelt's advisers had privately concluded that unemployment in America might never again fall below 6 million.

WHY DID IT HAPPEN ?

Capitalism at fault?

The fact that the West did not swiftly achieve full economic recovery was widely believed to show that capitalism as an economic system had failed. It was condemned as irrational, because people could see that factories closed and land lay idle while millions lacked the basic necessities of life. Left-wing groups in the United States called for "a scientifically planned economic system," in which factories and farms would be directed by the government to produce what people needed— "production for use instead of profit."

Nowadays, however, it is more common to see the failure to recover as a consequence of a breakdown in international cooperation, which undermined the capitalist system. For example, journalist Alan Shipman wrote in 2002: "Recovery was ... delayed because nations could not work together to rekindle activity, instead trying to revive their own economies by raising trade barriers and devaluing their currencies."

Socialist quotes in Anthony Badger, *The New Deal* (Macmillan, 1989); Alan Shipman, *The Globalization Myth* (Icon Books, 2002)

CHAPTER 6

A NEW CONFLICT

In September 1939, as a result of Nazi Germany's invasion of Poland, Britain and France declared war on Germany. World War II had begun. Two years later, in December 1941, Japan attacked the United States naval base at Pearl Harbor, Hawaii, bringing America into the war.

DEPRESSION AND WAR

The Depression had helped to bring nationalists and militarists to power in Germany and Japan, the major aggressors in the war. Once in power, their response to the situation had been to adopt totally nationalist economic policies. Seeking to become economically self-sufficient, rather than dependent on trade, they planned the conquest of other countries that had the resources they lacked. Germany's dictator, Adolf Hitler, envisioned conquering a large area to the east of Germany and exploiting it to provide food for Germans. The Japanese wanted to control Indonesia, the main source of Japan's oil supplies. Conquest also offered a more direct solution to economic problems, since a defeated country could be plundered for its wealth and its people used as slave labor.

THE END OF THE DEPRESSION

It can be said that the Depression both contributed to the causes of World War II, and was ended by it. In the United States, unemployment began falling sharply from 1939 onwards. Even before entering the war, America was, in Roosevelt's words, "the arsenal of democracy," supplying arms and food to Britain and its allies. By the time of Pearl Harbor in 1941, unemployment

A U.S. Army officer inspects new recruits, lined up in their civilian clothes, as America prepares for World War II. The entry of so many men into the armed forces sharply reduced unemployment, and equipping them for war gave industry a huge boost.

Having a good war

Many Americans, including farmers who had experienced poverty in the 1920s and 1930s, found themselves enjoying a new degree of prosperity, thanks to the war. A woman from rural Idaho remembered:

"As farm prices got better ... we and most other farmers went from a tarpaper shack to a new frame house with indoor plumbing. Now we had an electric stove instead of a woodburning one, and running water at the sink where we could do the dishes; and a hotwater heater ... We bought a vacuum cleaner too ... that was really wonderful!"

Quoted in David M. Kennedy, *Freedom from Fear* (Oxford University Press, 1999)

A factory in the Midwest turns out American B-24 Liberator bombers. Over 18,000 were manufactured during the war, just one example of the astonishing feats of industrial mass production that contributed to the Allied victory.

was down from 9 million in 1939 to 3 million. Once the United States entered the war, unemployment was replaced by a labor shortage. As the war industries boomed, workers were able to command higher wages. The availability of well-paid factory jobs attracted large numbers of poor farmers and farmworkers, many of them African Americans, to the cities. Women also broke into areas of industrial work that until then had been exclusively male. By 1943, it was not only the war industries that were booming but also the production of consumer goods, now being bought by workers with their rising wages. Between 1939 and 1945, American industrial output doubled.

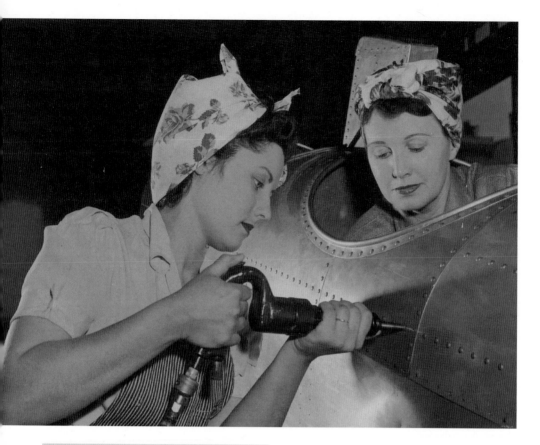

With so many men in the armed forces and new factories opening every week, American companies were forced to recruit women. When peace returned, most of them lost their jobs.

In Britain, too, unemployment had already fallen to 1 million by April 1940, and by the following year serious labor shortages were developing as the need to increase arms production coincided with the enrolling of millions of men and women into the armed forces. Government spending went up from around £1 billion in the last year of peace to almost £5 billion in 1941–42, giving a huge boost to the economy. In the struggle for survival, ideas about balancing government income and expenditure were abandoned.

WELCOME TO THE NEW WORLD

Determined that there would be no return to the Depression years, the United States, Britain, and their allies started drawing up plans for the postwar world economy even before the war ended. The nationalism of the Depression era would be replaced by internationalism, and instead of national economies being protected by tariffs, there would be free trade. A new organization, the United Nations, would ensure international cooperation instead of conflict. The Bretton Woods Agreement of 1944 set up institutions under the UN umbrella to give order and stability to the world economy. In the UN Charter, employment

TURNING POINTS IN HISTORY

The Bretton Woods Agreement

In July 1944, the American resort town of Bretton Woods in New Hampshire was host to 730 delegates from 44 countries who met to decide how the postwar world economy should be run. All equally determined that there should be no return to the Depression, they set up two key international institutions—the International Monetary Fund, to maintain stable exchange rates, and the International Bank for Reconstruction and Development (later to become the World Bank) to provide a stable source of capital investment to promote postwar economic recovery. The value of national currencies was to be fixed against the U.S. dollar, enabling the restoration of global free trade. The Bretton Woods agreement helped to establish a stable system of international trade and finance after the war. The fixing of currencies against the dollar lasted until 1971.

The United Nations Security Council meets in New York in 1946. The UN provided a useful framework for international cooperation, including the promotion of free trade and economic recovery. Despite the UN's best intentions, however, relations between the Soviet Union and the United States would soon turn hostile.

was listed as a fundamental human right—it was the responsibility of governments to prevent a return to mass unemployment.

By the end of the war, the United States was responsible for half of the world's total industrial output and was overwhelmingly the world's dominant economy. While in America industries had expanded and living standards had risen, industrialized countries on both sides in the war—including Germany, Japan, Britain, and the Soviet Union—had suffered large-scale destruction. In stark contrast to its position after World War I, after 1945 the United States accepted the role of leader of the capitalist world economy. This was confirmed in 1947 when, under the Marshall Plan, the United States provided the money to help Western European countries recover from the effects of the war. America's leaders understood that a revival of the world

In contrast to the Depression years, 1950s America was a place of prosperity and optimism. These women buying lunch at a drive-in restaurant in Los Angeles in 1951 are enjoying the advantages of virtually full employment and swiftly rising average incomes.

economy served not only America's economic interests, but also its political interests, since promoting prosperity was seen as a means of preventing the spread of communism.

BOOM TIMES RETURN

The 1950s and 1960s saw a sustained economic boom in the major industrial countries of Western Europe, the United States, and Japan. Growth rates exceeded all expectations, unemployment was low, trade flourished, and average incomes rose steeply. Economic and social policies varied from country to country, but all built to some degree on the lessons learned from the Depression. In both Europe and the United States, for

example, governments supported agricultural prices by purchasing surplus farm produce or paying farmers to keep land out of production.

FUTURE IMPERFECT

It came as a shock to people of the 1970s, to whom the Depression was part of the distant past, that financial troubles were again on the horizon. In 1971, a weak dollar put an end to the dollar-based fixed exchange rates established at Bretton Woods. Throughout the decade, a combination of high inflation and rising unemployment continued to rock industrial economies. The response was a return to the economic strategies of the pre-Depression era. Governments such as that of British prime minister Margaret Thatcher in the 1980s went back to the ideal of balancing budgets and cutting government spending. In the 1990s, the United States abandoned

Another Depression

The matter of whether a world slump on the scale of the Depression could happen again has rarely been off the academic debating schedule. Economic historian Harold James points out that for some optimists the "Depression was a once-only event, one that derived essentially from the consequences of the First World War." Since such a war could never happen again, he argues, neither would such a Depression.

Historians Kevin O'Rourke and Jeffery Williamson, however, see the Depression as having resulted from a "globalization backlash," meaning a nationalist reaction by key countries against the pre-1914 global economy, which they saw as harming their national interests. In this view, the globalized economy of the twenty-first century, with its inequalities and injustices, might again breed hostile reaction from governments, leading to a Depression-style breakdown in world trade.

Harold James, *The End of Globalization* (Harvard, 2001); Kevin O'Rourke and Jeffery Williamson, *Globalization and History* (MIT Press, Cambridge Massachusetts, 1999)

much of the New Deal welfare system.

The next few years saw periodic fears of a return to the Depression. In the 1980s, unemployment rose in many countries. There were occasional stock market crashes that matched or even exceeded the Great Crash of 1929—notably in 1987 and at the start of the twenty-first century. In 2007, a "credit crunch" resulting from the overselling of mortgages shook banks and finance companies the world over and brought down some of the best-known banks in America. Critics were not slow to make comparisons to the 1930s, but it seemed that another Great Depression had been averted—perhaps because the memory of the original still stood as a dire warning of what human misery might result if the global economy were ever really to fall apart.

Franklin Roosevelt himself would perhaps be disappointed to find that most of the welfare system he created had been abolished by the end of the twentieth century. Nevertheless, the Franklin D. Roosevelt Memorial in Washington D.C. is today visited by thousands who respect the memory of the architect of the New Deal.

GREAT DEPRESSION TIMELINE

1914–18

World War I fundamentally disrupts the world economy

1919

Peace treaty signed at Versailles imposes reparations payments on Germany

1921

Unemployment in Britain tops 2 million

1923

Hyperinflation in Germany destroys the value of the German currency

1929

March: Herbert Hoover is inaugurated as U.S. President

October 24: Share prices on the U.S. stock market crash on Black Thursday

October 29: Black Tuesday, the worst single day of the stock market crash

1930

Unemployment rises to 5 million in the United States; over 1,000 U.S. banks shut down

1931

Unemployment rises to over 5 million in Germany and over 3 million in Britain

1932

U.S. unemployment rises to 12–13 million; Franklin D. Roosevelt wins U.S. presidential election

1933

January 30: Nazi Party leader Adolf Hitler becomes Chancellor of Germany

March–June: The first 100 days of Roosevelt's presidency lay the foundation for the New Deal

July: A World Economic Conference in London breaks up without agreement

1933–35

Drought and soil erosion in Oklahoma and neighboring states create the Dust Bowl

1935

Radical measures of the Second New Deal are introduced, including the Social Security Act

1936

October: The Jarrow March of unemployed men brings a petition to the British parliament

November: Roosevelt wins a landslide victory in presidential election

1937

Unemployment rises sharply again in the United States; a wave of sit-down strikes sweeps the United States; the Farm Security Administration is created to help the rural poor

1939

In September, World War II begins

1944

In July, the Bretton Woods Conference produces international agreement on how to organize a postwar world economy

GLOSSARY

balanced budget A budget in which a government's spending equals its income.

boom Sharp rise in economic activity.

broker An agent who buys and sells on someone else's behalf.

capitalism An economic system based on private ownership of business and trade.

communism A system in which most or all economic life is controlled by the state.

consumer goods Products sold to people for personal use.

devaluing Reducing the value of one currency when exchanged for another

free (or private) enterprise Economic system based on the pursuit of profit by individuals or companies.

free trade International trade without excessive tariffs or obstructive regulations.

global (or world) economy A single interlocking system of trade and investment.

growth rates The speed at which an economy expands.

hyperinflation A rise in prices so steep that a currency becomes virtually valueless.

inflation A rise in prices and fall in the value of a currency.

isolationism Tendency in the United States to avoid involvement in alliances or other entanglements with foreign countries.

liberal capitalism A form of capitalism in which governments exercise an absolute minimum of control over economic activity.

price-fixing agreement An arrangement between competing businesses not to sell goods below a certain price.

shares A form of investment in business: people buy shares in companies and in theory make a profit if the company expands and increases in value.

speculation Buying and selling shares in search of a quick profit, regardless of the true value of companies.

stock market Place in which shares are traded.

tariff A tax imposed on imported goods.

Wall Street U.S. stock market.

FURTHER INFORMATION

Books:

Blumenthal, Karen. *Six Days in October: The Stock Market Crash of 1929*. New York: Atheneum, 2002.

Cooper, Michael L. *Dust to Eat: Drought and Depression in the 1930s*. New York: Clarion, 2004.

Gow, Mary. *The Stock Market Crash of 1929: Dawn of the Great Depression*. Berkeley Heights, NJ: Enslow, 2003.

Grant, R.G. *The Great Depression*. Hauppage, NY: Barron's, 2003.

Gunderson, Cory. *The Great Depression*. Edina, MN: ABDO, 2004.

Wroble, Lisa A. *The New Deal and the Great Depression in American History*. Springfield, NJ: Enslow, 2002.

Web Sites:

Documenting America (http://memory.loc.gov/ammem/fsowhome. html)

New Deal Network (http://www.newdeal.feri.org/)

PBS: Surviving the Dust Bowl (http://www.pbs.org/wgbh/americanexperience/ films/dustbowl/)

Publisher's note to educators and parents: Our editors have carefully reviewed these Web sites to ensure that they are suitable for students. Many Web sites change frequently, however, and we cannot guarantee that a site's future contents will continue to meet our high standards of quality and educational value. Be advised that students should be closely supervised whenever they access the Internet.

INDEX

Numbers in **bold** refer to pictures

African Americans 11, **12**, 37, 38, 41
agriculture 8, 12, 15, **18**, 22, 23, 27, 28, 37, 44
arms production 32, 40, **41**
Austria 22

"bank holidays" 27
banks and banking 13, 14, **15**, 18, 21, 22, 27, 28, 43, 45
Black Thursday 16
Bonus Army protest 24, **25**
boom 10, 11, 13, 17, 44
Brazil 20
Bretton Woods Agreement 42, 43
Britain 4, 5, 7, 8, 9, **19**, 20, **21**, 22, 34, **35**, 36, 39, 40, 42, 43, 44
budgets 20, 23, 25, 26, 44

capitalism 33, 39
cars **10**, 39
charities **16**, 24
Chile 19
civil war 6
Civilian Conservation Corps (CCC) **29**
Civilian Works Administration (CWA) 29
colonies (*see also* empire, British) 8
communism 5, 6, 33
consumer goods 10, 12, 18, 41
Coolidge, President Calvin 11
cotton farming **12**, 27
Crash, Great 13, 14, 15, 16, 17
crashes, stock market (*see also* Crash, Great) 45
currencies 6, 9, 20, 22, 34, 36, 39, 43

Dawes Plan 9
debt 5, 12, 13
Dust Bowl **36**, 38

economic growth (*see also* recovery) 4, 9, 10
electrical goods 10, 18, 38, **39**
empire, British **34**, 36
Empire State Building **11**
evictions 24

Farm Security Administration (FSA) 38
free trade 34, 42, 43
fruit-pickers **37**

Germany 4, 5, 6, 7, 9, 19, 20, 21, 22, **31**, 34, 35, 40
Gold Standard 9, 21, 22

Hitler, Adolf **31**, 40
"hobos" 24
Hoover, President Herbert 11, 17, **22**, 23, 24
"Hoovervilles" **23**
hyperinflation 6, **7**

industrial production 4, 5, 7, 8, 10, 19, 20, 33, 36, 37, 39, 41, 42
industrialization 4, 33
inflation 6, 7
Invergordon mutiny 21
investment 4, 9, 13, 14, 19
isolationism 9

Japan 20, 40
Jarrow **35**, 36
Jews 32

labor shortages 41, 42
League of Nations **9**
loans 13, 18, 38

MacDonald, P. M., Ramsay 22
Marshall Plan 43
Marx, Harpo 15

National Recovery Administration (NRA) 27, **28**, 30
Nazi Party **20**, 21, 31, 32
New Deal 26, **28**, **29**, **30**, 31, 32
New Zealand **34**

overproduction 8, 12

"panhandlers" 24
policies, government 20, 23, 25, 26–32, 34, 35, 40, 44
poverty 5, 8, 11, 12, 18, **23**, 24, **37**, **38**
prohibition 26
protests **21**, 24, **25**, **35**

recovery 19, 27, 28, 34, 43
relief 24, 28, 29
reparations 6, 7, 9

Roosevelt, Franklin D. 25, 26, **27**, 28, 29, 30, **31**, 32, 33, **45**
Ruhr, occupation of 6
Russia 4, 5, 6

Second New Deal 30
share prices 13, 14, 15, 16, 17
Smoot-Hawley Tariff Act 23
Social Security Act 31
Soviet Union 6, **32**
Spartacists **5**
speculation 13, 15, 16
spending, government 20, 22, 23, 25, 26, 32, 42, 44
Stalin, Joseph 33
stock market 13, 14, 16, 17, 45
strikes 6, **38**

tariffs 22, 23
taxes 20, 22, 23, 25
technological progress 38, 39
Tennessee Valley Authority (TVA) **30**
trade (*see also* free trade) 22, 34, 35, 36, 38, 39, 40, 42, 44
trade unions 31, 32, 38

unemployment 4, 7, **16**, 18, **19**, 20, **24**, 28, 29, 30, 31, 32, 33, 34, 36, 37, 40, 41, 42, 44, 45
United Nations 42, **43**
United States 4, 5, 6, 7, 8, 9, **10**–18, 19, 22, **23**, **24**, **25**, 26–30, 31, 34, **36–37**, **38**, 39, **40**, **41**, 42, 43, 44, 45

Versailles, Treaty of **6**

Wagner Act 31
Wall Street **13**, **14**, 17
wealth 11, **44**
women **24**, 32, **42**
work programs 28, 29, 31
World War I **4**, 9
World War II 40, 41